Wakefield Press

ARCADIAN ADELAIDE

Arcadian
ADELAIDE

Thistle Anderson

with an essay on the historical context by

DEREK WHITELOCK

Foreword by Katie Spain

**Wakefield
Press**

Wakefield Press
16 Rose Street
Mile End
South Australia 5031
wakefieldpress.com.au

First published by Wakefield Press, 1985
This new edition published 2020

Cover and pages designed by Liz Nicholson, Wakefield Press
Typeset by Michael Deves, Wakefield Press

ISBN 978 1 74305 618 9

 A catalogue record for this
book is available from the
National Library of Australia

 Wakefield Press thanks
Coriole Vineyards for
continued support

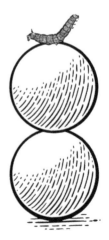

Dedication

*"To any kindred spirit whom duty
may compel to live in Adelaide, and who,
living there, suffers as we suffer."*

THISTLE ANDERSON

CONTENTS

FOREWORD

Katie Spain

Oh, how wonderful it would be to step back in time for a face-to-face chat with Scottish-born actress and satirical writer Thistle Anderson. As interviews go, she'd be a journalist's dream; well-travelled, articulate, witty, and gut-wrenchingly honest.

I'd give my writing hand for an encounter with the author of *Arcadian Adelaide*. Thistle (otherwise known as Mrs Herbert Fisher) published her terse little pamphlet in 1905 and by all accounts it caused quite the stir in sleepy old Adelaide. It's a ripper of a read.

'Adelaide, known to all intelligent people as the City of Juvenile Depravity,' she wrote. 'And to the less enlightened as the City of Churches.' Ouch.

Thistle described *Arcadian Adelaide* as a playful skit but it rocked sensitive South Australian readers to the core. With a firm hand, a sharp tongue, and a nib dripping in satire she dissected the city she temporarily called home (or 'ripped it a new one' as most would say today).

Fast forward to 2020, the year of the global COVID pandemic. A time when bright (and not-so-bright) young things flock to Instagram account *Shit Adelaide* for their daily dose of satirical Adelaide-inspired excrement. Thistle was the whistle blower of the early 1900s. The *Shit Adelaide* of the olden days. In her heyday, the pen (and a sense of humour) were mightier than the sword and the keyboard.

These days, the closest we get to her delightfully deprecating drivel is ABC Radio's Peter Goers during one of his anti-Burnside rants or Barry Humphries in full Dame Edna Everage flight. After all, it was Dame Edna who said, 'Never be afraid to laugh at yourself, after all, you could be missing out on the joke of the century.'

Thistle wasn't laughing at herself, she was laughing at everyone else.

She took no prisoners when explaining why she disliked the City of Churches. 'Adelaide has crushed my youthful ambitions, and, possibly, narrowed my ideas,' she wrote.

Arcadian Adelaide was published just a few years after women's suffrage in Australia – led by South Australia in 1894. Suddenly, women had the right to vote at federal elections and stand for the federal Parliament. Imagine! It was enough to send tongues flapping. Then along came Thistle. She was bold and outspoken in a way few women were back then. Adelaide was home and she wanted out. Her bite was fierce and left venom in its wake. No one was safe, particularly the ladies of Adelaide (whom she referred to as cats) and the men (the unsightly, unkempt, unfashionable lot of 'em).

These days, thanks to the anonymity of the Internet, everyone is a critic but few do it with the pasquinade and flippant bon mot displayed by Thistle.

Time travel looks to be a way off yet, but should technological advances one day provide the chance for resurrection, I've compiled a list of questions – just in case.

What would Thistle make of the city we now call home? Did the 21st century mark a coming of age or would she still describe our existence as, 'A distressing state of semi-civilization?'

What would she think of annual arts extravaganzas the Adelaide Fringe and Adelaide Festival, or the impressive renovation of the historic Her Majesty's Theatre? 'Adelaide has a theatre and a music hall,' she wrote in 1905. 'The former is open for about four months in the year, and generally spells financial disaster to enterprising managers.'

I'd like to think she'd have a soft spot for the late Don Dunstan. South Australia's 35th Premier dragged Adelaide (kicking and screaming) into the modern world. Under his progressive guidance, society had a facelift – or a lobotomy of sorts. Aboriginal land rights were recognised, homosexuality decriminalised, the first female judge appointed, universal suffrage enacted, multiculturalism encouraged, public education and health systems reformed, Rundle Mall established (though she'd abhor those giant silver balls and towering pigeon sculpture), heritage buildings protected, and unwavering support injected into the arts (particularly the Adelaide Festival Centre, State Theatre Company, and the South Australian Film Corporation). Dunstan got us permission to dine al fresco, damn it. I also think she'd dig his style.

On the flipside, Thistle would probably lament the demise of Holden's manufacturing operations, disapprove of cuts to the state's arts budget, and grumble about housing prices.

What would she make of the glistening North Terrace structure we call the RAH? One can only imagine her vitriol over ambulance ramping. How would she feel about the state's handling of COVID? No doubt she'd demand we close international and domestic borders. After all, who'd want to come here anyway?

What about Adelaide's unwanted status as the nation's methamphetamine capital? We've got waste-water data gathered by the Australian Criminal

Intelligence Commission in 2018 to thank for that one – in other words, our wee. Maybe she was on to something all those years ago. 'Melbourne, with approximately a population of 494,129, has seven opium dens; while Adelaide, with a population 162,261, has eight,' she wrote.

In 2013 News.com.au used the first coherent result in Google's auto-complete options (the predictive text that shows up when you type in a search term) to show what people really think of Australia. It wasn't flattering. The result when you typed in Adelaide was, 'Adelaide is a hole.' Sydney didn't fare much better. 'Sydney is expensive and stupid.'

Thistle would get a kick out of that but would she nod in brisk approval to hear that Adelaide clocked in as one of *Lonely Planet*'s top 10 cities to visit in 2014? Or that Colonel Light's vision was named Australia's most liveable city in the 2013 Property Council's national survey? What about *Condé Nast Traveler*'s declaration that Rads is one of the friendliest cities in the world due to its 'chill coastal vibe and first-rate natural wines'? Such claims are a South Australian Tourism Commission's wet dream.

Speaking of beverages and social trends, Thistle had great things to say about South Australia's fruit industry, but her disdain for our wine and the people who made it was tangible. Sure, our plonk wasn't a patch on the stuff coming out of France in the early 1900s but things have come a long way.

In 2016 Adelaide was named a Great Wine Capital and you can't go a day without hearing someone make reference to the small bar scene and inner city 'vibrancy'. What would Thistle think of the small bars full of hip young things with deep pockets and an insatiable thirst for natural wine? Listen hard enough and you'll hear her scoff from the grave over news that a six-litre Imperial bottle of 2013 Penfolds Grange Shiraz sold for $58,250 during the 2019 Barossa Wine Auction. Don't even get her started on the state of affairs on Hindley Street at 3 am on a Saturday morning, or the ongoing tram debacle.

'So much has been said, and written, about Adelaide's tram-cars, that any reference to the subject is of necessity boring, yet they are the worst evil (worst, because, apparently, irremediable) in all Australasia,' she scrawled in 1905.

I think modern-day Thistle would find plenty to love about postcode 5000 and its surrounding areas – and even more to hate. She was an example that we should never rest on our laurels. Like most people who left Adelaide to experience the world, I get a thrill every time I jet off to faraway places, and an even bigger thrill when the plane hits the tarmac upon my return. The jacaranda-lined streets are home again now and Dorothy was right. There's no place like home. There's also nothing like the power of the written word. Or progress. Here's to people like Thistle Anderson; to speaking out, stirring emotions, and holding a mirror to our faces and surrounds – all in the hope of making it a better place to live. Or, at the very least, inciting a chuckle.

A crowd lines the centre of King William Street to see the Eight Hours Day procession pass by. A horse tram can be seen in the procession. c. 1895
[SLSA B 8844]

Yours faithfully,
Thistle Anderson

ARCADIAN ADELAIDE.

BY

THISTLE ANDERSON

(MRS. HERBERT FISHER).

———◆———

Author of " Barenski," " Verses at Random," &c.

ADELAIDE :
MODERN PRINTING COMPANY, TWIN STREET,

1905.

AUTHOR'S NOTE

SOME Adelaide residents—and especially a section of the Press—have accused me of bitterness, and believe this book to have been written from personal motives, with a desire to be malicious. I can only repeat what I stated in the Foreword to my first edition—that no malice is intended. To that statement I add my regret for possible offence caused to any of my personal friends.

The book was written merely as a playful skit, just as T. W. H. Crossland wrote "The Unspeakable Scot". Scotland took Mr. Crossland's book as it was intended, and I expected Adelaide to do me the same justice.

That all the public do not misinterpret my motives, is shown by the sale of the book—it has succeeded (if one may judge its success by its selling capacity) beyond my most sanguine expectations, and I cordially thank the public for their support.

THISTLE ANDERSON, 1905

AUTHOR'S FOREWORD

IT has been suggested to me, O people of Adelaide, that, should any of you deign to glance through these pages, you will misunderstand them—that is to say, you will believe them to have been written with malicious intent. What the public may think or say troubles me little, but for the benefit of one or two persons here who merit consideration, I emphatically declare that this is not so. Adelaide has crushed my youthful ambitions, and, possibly, narrowed my ideas—and you, her people, have done your best (by force of example, and other methods) to root out any broad or human sentiment that was in me. So that I have nothing for which to thank you, and I owe you nothing—not even the merest courtesy.

But the feeling of bitterness that characterised my first unhappy moments here has long since passed, and there is left only resignation, and perhaps a faint hope that some day I may sail "beyond the sunset and the baths of all the Western stars" forever. It may be argued that I have taken a near and dear—very near and very dear—relation from among you, and to that my only answer can be that he did not choose his birthplace, and that it is his misfortune—a misfortune which, however, has happily produced no lasting effect.

Thistle Anderson.

"STRAMSHALL,"
NORTH ADELAIDE, *April 12th, 1905.*

PART I

THE PLACE

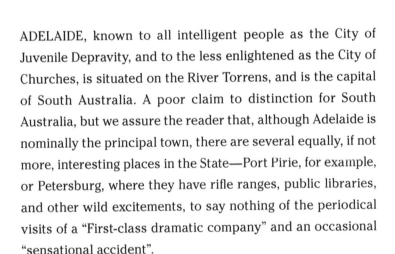

Chapter I

THE HOLY VILLAGE

ADELAIDE, known to all intelligent people as the City of Juvenile Depravity, and to the less enlightened as the City of Churches, is situated on the River Torrens, and is the capital of South Australia. A poor claim to distinction for South Australia, but we assure the reader that, although Adelaide is nominally the principal town, there are several equally, if not more, interesting places in the State—Port Pirie, for example, or Petersburg, where they have rifle ranges, public libraries, and other wild excitements, to say nothing of the periodical visits of a "First-class dramatic company" and an occasional "sensational accident".

The Village itself consists of a main street (Rundle Street) and several lesser streets, and is surrounded by Park Lands, which, unlike Adelaide itself, are quite useful—in that they supply the homeless wanderer with sleeping accommodation free. In early morning they are almost as thickly peopled as

Sydney Domain, and afford a refuge to burglars, sundowners, unemployed and other unfortunates. We have camped out ourselves when fishing, and we think the Park Lands are green enough, at certain seasons, to offer every inducement to quiet rest.

OUTWARDLY, Adelaide is intensely respectable—that is to say, the inhabitants go to church regularly, and think it extremely wrong to play cards for money. They are ostentatious in their charity, but it goes very little below the surface. Their ideas are, for the most part, about as broad as Blondin's wire, and their cardinal virtues are Religious Belief and Conventionality. Briefly summed up, the creed of Adelaide so-called Society runs:—

King William Road looking north across the River Torrens. Spires of churches in North Adelaide rise above the treeline. Elder Park and the Rotunda are in the foreground. A horse drawn bus is driving up towards North Terrace. c. 1882–86. [SLSA B 3124]

"I believe in Lewis Cohen, Mayor of Adelaide, and in Sir George LeHunte (or any other man), Governor of South Australia, from whom much hospitality may be expected. He was appointed in England, and ascended into Government House. From thence he shall issue many invitations. I believe in the social laws, in much going to Church, in doing to others as they would do unto you if they could, in the charity that will be beneficial to our social position, and in the Life of the Everlasting. Amen."

Of real charity there is little, as will be shown later on.

Several well-known pillars of Adelaide have been more than generous, and have showered gifts on the village—notably a School of Mines, Statues, wings to Hospitals, Lions to the Zoo, etc.—not forgetting an elderly lady who paid for building nearly half of a famous church. Rumor hath it that the youthful curate promptly offered her his hand and heart, presumably in gratitude for her generosity.

So much for charity in Adelaide.

The Village is less holy than might be supposed, for Melbourne, with approximately a population of 494,129, has seven opium dens; while Adelaide, with a population 162,261, has eight. Then, too, it is pretty generally admitted that, in proportion to its size, Adelaide has more prostitution and more young girls on its streets than any other city in Australasia. Many women of the unfortunate class in Adelaide begin their wretched profession at the early age of thirteen or fourteen. Most of the Village's newspapers have, to do them justice, militated against this evil—but unsuccessfully. The author knows of two local cases in which a mother deliberately trained her daughter to her own degrading career. It may be argued that similar cases abound in every city, but the reader must remember that Adelaide has clothed itself in a self-constituted halo of excessive virtue. This is not a treatise on morality—it is not Adelaide's lack of morality to which I am objecting, but her lack of sincerity, to my mind a far greater evil. Be a little more humble, ye people of Adelaide, try to remember that your hills are not the greenest, or your morals the cleanest, or your shops the brightest in the whole world—and if you cannot bring yourselves to remember these things, then bear in mind that your wines are the worst ever made, that some of you are passing plain to look upon, and that you have acquired a world-wide fame for your cruelty to animals—especially horses.

Adelaide is justly famed for the beauty of her Botanical Gardens, and the antiquity of her tramway system, and it is on these two facts that her main claim to distinction is based. To be sure there is no antiquity in Adelaide *except* the trams (and the tailors!)—and this is distinctly a pity. Next to the downright, thorough civilization of Paris or London, the happiest state is primitive rusticity; but here, a desire to be civilized, coupled with an inability to carry out the idea, have resulted in a distressing state of semi-civilization, which is most unpleasant. Things which should be old, are young, and *vice versa*. For instance, the shops are amazingly old, and the buildings aggressively new, which is a pity, for it is the privilege of shops to be modern, just as it is the privilege of buildings to be ancient.

The daily excitements of Adelaide are the coming of letters, and the going of the Melbourne express—the fascination of the latter will be readily understood, when it is

The Melbourne Express 'always *leaves* Adelaide on time'
Adelaide Railway Station, c. 1900 [SLSA B-27154]

remembered that it forms the principal link between Adelaide and civilization. To be sure, the letters are as behind-hand as the local divorce law, but this fact merely shows an excusable disinclination on the part of the engine driver to revisit Adelaide, for, be it observed, the express always *leaves* the Village at the appointed time.

Adelaide has a theatre and a music hall—the former is open for about four months in the year, and generally spells financial disaster to enterprising managers. The latter, when not devoted to the lectures of the Reverend Henry Howard, revels in biograph entertainments, occasionally varied by a good variety show, which latter is, need we say, but little patronised.

The climate of Adelaide is good in spots—dust in summer, and hot winds—and in winter, much rain. The Hills, of which residents are so proud, are deluged with rain for nearly six months in the year, and for nearly all the remaining six they are burnt so brown as to lose all semblance to anything but volcanic rocks. Still, I have enjoyed glorious spring and autumn days in those hills—days that have lent themselves to picnics, which were generally made merry by the presence of persons not of Adelaide.

Apart from the tram-steeds the Adelaide horseflesh is superior, and takes many prizes, and I have a few delightful equine adventures—difficult to master, to look upon, and recollections of of horses splendid exciting to drive. Many of these emanated from Hill & Co.'s stables, an excellent institution of its kind, where both horses and men are of good calibre, but, unfortunately, not smartly turned out—to be smart is to transgress the social etiquette of the Village.

And there are other bright memories of Adelaide, notably Adams, a merry soul from Hill and Co.'s stables, who taught present scribe the delights of four-in-hand driving, thereby offering endless facilities for desecrating the virtuous Adelaide Sabbath. To Adams, a vote of thanks! And a thrill of real enthusiasm when I remember those crisp June mornings, the thud of the bloods' hoofs in the frosty stillness, the scent of the fragrant earth—peace in my heart, sunshine abroad, and, for the time, the petty mortifications of my surroundings forgotten. Ah! Those were good days, and they stand out from the rest; but, alas! They are too few to compensate for other more frequent, and less enjoyable, days that must be endured.

Other attractions of the Village are a gallery of pictures, for the most part badly chosen; much statuary, which looks cheap, and was in reality expensive; and several tea-rooms. These latter are, of course, unlicensed, the tea is inferior, the cakes stale, and all the cups cracked, so they are not to be recommended.

Altogether, as a place of education Adelaide falls far short of the mark; as a place of amusement it is hopeless, and as a village—well, it is tolerably clean, and comparatively healthy.

King William Street, Adelaide. 1902. [SLSA B 72777]

Chapter II

LIVING ACCOMMODATION

THERE are numberless licensed places in Adelaide, where drink, varying in quality and unlimited in quantity, may be obtained, and there is one Hotel—the South Australian. It is distinctly promising, and I am glad it does not call itself "The Adelaide" Hotel, because that would damn it eternally— "South Australian" is so much more comprehensive. Whatever small element of rank and fashion there is in the Village, congregates in those spacious halls and early Victorian reception-rooms—early-Victorian in the stiff-backed dignity of the furniture, and the scarcity of carpets. Moreover, one occasionally meets there persons who have been rash enough to leave better places to visit Adelaide. Let us be charitable, and hope that sternest duty brings them here. Surely no other motive could induce their presence? And let us remark, as a warning to others contemplating the same folly (especially theatrical managers), that if they come here in the hope of amusing, or being amused, bitter will be their disappointment. Those who visit the city of many white sepulchres on business, are forgiven—those who come on pleasure bent should be relegated to asylums for the insane. However, should they remain here long enough, the insanity will follow.

The hotel itself is really charming—the staff is good, which is not surprising when one remembers that most of the employés hail from other places. The fact that *is* surprising is that they can be content to work and serve so long here. This, however, is a tribute to the untiring kindness of the proprietress and the manager.

The imposing South Australian Hotel, Adelaide's 'only' hotel with 'class'.
South Australian Hotel, North Terrace, c. 1900 [SLSA PRG-280-1-4-195]

To keep servants long in any part of the world is both creditable and clever—to keep them long in Adelaide shows positive genius.*

The liquor in the only hotel is passing good, save that it gives preference to South Australian Wines, which is criminal. But of Australian wine, more in another chapter. The hotel has, as I have said before, a charming proprietress, a capable manager and a splendid staff, and it has other virtues of a first-class hostelry. A substantial improvement might be effected by weeding out some of the permanent and usual boarders (mainly female) modernizing the rooms a little, and building vast quantities of additional bathrooms. Then add to the stock some good French Burgundy, some three-star Brandy that isn't Hennessy, some Dewar's Imperial Whisky, and a greater variety of liqueurs, and the "South Australian" would be a veritable oasis in the desert of Adelaide. As it is, it rivals the best hotels in the Southern Hemisphere, and to all who contemplate residence in Adelaide, we issue this warning—don't be induced to stay elsewhere. (N.B.—This advertisement is not paid for.)

---

* I except my own servants to this rule—no genius is exercised to keep them, because none is required—as they, with one exception, come from Melbourne, they have some faint idea of their duties—THE AUTHOR.

Of the other licensed houses there is little to be said; they are mainly patronized by country farmers, who are uninteresting people at best, and therefore deserving of little consideration. I once had the misfortune to spend a few days at one of these so-called Hotels on North Terrace, and amongst many minor inconveniences one heard the screams of delirious patients at the Hospital, the yells of the inmates of North Terrace Asylum, and the roar of the wild beasts from the not far-distant Zoo—it was distinctly a thrilling experience.

The staircase of the South Australian Hotel, North Terrace, Adelaide, c. 1902. [SLSA PRG-733-443]

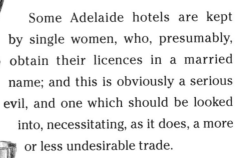

Some Adelaide hotels are kept by single women, who, presumably, obtain their licences in a married name; and this is obviously a serious evil, and one which should be looked into, necessitating, as it does, a more or less undesirable trade.

There are boarding-houses, too, many of them enormously respectable, and occasionally they are fortunate enough to have some of their rooms occupied. They are much the same as other boarding houses all over the world—that is to say, food indifferent, drinks difficult to obtain, and attendance nil. I have never lived in an Adelaide boarding-house, but I once lunched at one. The rats had eaten most of my hostess' clothes, which wasn't surprising. Having sampled the food, one couldn't blame those discriminating rodents for preferring the boarders' garments.

There are many more or less charitable institutions which provide living accommodation, in some cases free, but these appear to be inaccessible to the people who really need them. At the "Queen's Maternity Home," for instance, the marriage lines are the necessary qualification for admittance. No doubt the institution is excellent in its way, but Charity cannot draw distinctions of that sort, and so the home in question

simply misses the primary object of such places.[†] There are also Benovelent, Destitute, and Blind Asylums, and several asylums for lunatics. The latter are, I understand, fairly well filled—which is easily understood.

Flats, most desirable of modern conveniences, are as yet unheard of in Adelaide, which shows a deplorable neglect of personal comfort—indeed, a lamentable ignorance of all comfortable living accommodation is manifest. A flat comprises the largest amount of comfort in the smallest possible space—may the deserving originator of the scheme be blessed or sainted. May undeserving Adelaide never know the blessings of such luxury.

The dwelling houses are, for the most part, cheaply built, badly fitted, and execrably furnished—there are a few notable exceptions, but these mostly err in the opposite direction, being lavishly vulgar in their gaudy upholsterings. Inwardly, Adelaide cannot esteem cleanliness a cardinal virtue, judging by the bathrooms in most of the available houses. A furnished house is very rarely to be had, and the few I have seen would preclude any desirable tenant from taking them. Ugh! The cheap and nasty furniture, china dogs, gaudy wall papers and architectural horrors of the Adelaide house! To those

---

[†] A small sum of money is paid by patients, according to their means, but the home is distinctly a charity, and calls itself one.— THE AUTHOR

who must sojourn here, and who cannot afford the expensive seclusion of the only hotel—bring your beds on your back, or bring a tent and camp in the park lands, for woe unto ye who trust to the doubtful hospitality of the village boarding-houses, or of the "house to let." We doubt if it is possible to be really comfortable here—certainly to be even tolerably comfortable, it is necessary to select—no, to bring—one's own furniture, wall papers and other house trapping.

Chapter III
THE TRAM CARS

Q.—"What is the difference between the Adelaide trams and the Adelaide street lights?"
A.—"One has a set o' lean horses, and the other has acetylene lamps!"

SO much has been said, and written, about Adelaide's tram-cars, that any reference to the subject is of necessity boring, yet they are the worst evil (worst, because, apparently, irremediable) in all Australasia, and the system is a disgrace to any community calling itself civilized, much less *Christian! Christian!* Save the mark!

In the *Advertiser* some months back appeared a letter signed "M. B. S.", written by a globe-trotter visiting the Village. He says—"I have been all over the world, and have never seen such cruelty to horses as here ... not even in Paris, where animals are not respected at all." No one can dispute "M. B. S's"

THE COLISEUM
TUM

The Bee Hive corner building dominates in this busy city street scene, taken just after five o'clock in the afternoon. In the foreground a man holds the horses as people wait to board a horse tram, soon to be superceded by the new electric trams which are seen passing along King William Street, 1909. [SLSA B-3532] statement. The facts are hideous. The company's shares are held by bloated—*very* bloated—property-holders. Of course they draw eight per cent or so, and, being essentially Adelaidean in their instincts, they want no change—they are satisfied.

It is unnecessary to dwell on the inconvenience to, and discomfort of, passengers—any discomfort they get I am inclined to think they deserve—and I speak solely from the standpoint of the ill-used horse. The cars are frequently overcrowded, the animals badly fed and mercilessly driven, and often in summer the miserable brutes fall dead. I have seen as many as three die within a fortnight on the hill near the Children's Hospital. It is pitiful, and if some of the so-called Christians of Adelaide employed a little less theory and a good deal more practice, some remedy might be effected. I am thankful to say that I have never ridden in one of these cars. May I die if ever I add to the burden of those unfortunate horses, or the wealth of those bloated shareholders! I am no ardent pedestrian, but a thousand times rather would I walk than participate in such brutal ill-usage of one of the noblest animals in the scheme of creation. Christians, forsooth! Christ, the gentlest and kindest of men, would never have countenanced such cruelty, and yet Adelaide is a Christian village, infested with Churchianity.

I would suggest that the promoters of this tramway system be boiled to slow music, the shareholders be mutilated, the drivers be put to a more Christian trade—or suffer the punishment of their unintelligence—and the youthful fare-collectors taught to espouse a nobler cause.

* * * * *

There are other modes of transit in the Village—one or two buses, some dilapidated machines called carettes, and some four-wheeled cabs. Some of the drivers of said four-wheelers treat their horses less brutally than does the tramway company, and therefore they deserve to make a living.

There are also several hansoms striving to earn a more or less honest crust under the frightful stigma of "not quite respectable—hardly correct!" To these we wish better days—the drivers are civil, the horses well fed, and the cabs fairly modern. Especially does one Fisher (no relation to the author) deserve to succeed, he having a decent intelligence, and a hansom worthy a better fate than Adelaide!

PART II

THE INHABITANTS

'The Men' of the Colonel Light Memorial Executive Committee, 1905.
[SLSA B 2367]

Chapter I
THE MEN

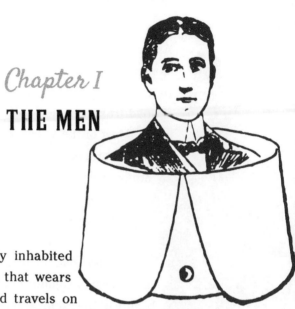

ADELAIDE is largely inhabited by the type of man that wears celluloid collars, and travels on coastal boats—to be sure there are a few male inhabitants who have neither qualification, but these are mainly bankrupt, and therefore do not count. It is fairly safe to assume their bankruptcy is due to their contempt for celluloid collars, and their disregard of Adelaide's social laws, combined, in many cases, with a large devotion to Bacchus.

Edward Lauri, when in Adelaide recently, remarked that the local men were the best caricature-types he had ever seen. "They nearly all look exactly alike," he said, "and they never change! In another five years they will look just as they look to-day. They are now wearing the same shaped hats, collars, and ties, and the same suits of clothes that they wore when I was here eighteen months ago!"

Assuming this statement to be true, it will be understood that they are not very exhilarating to meet—always excepting the bankrupts we alluded to before, some of whom are gay young bucks. Most of the Village's male population have married barmaids, nurses, or money, so the social atmosphere is not as high as it might be. They grow weird hirsute adornments in the shape of beards and whiskers. The only men who grow a self-respecting moustache are the coachmen, and with them it is an unnecessary adjunct, detracting much from the beauty of their appearance. Certainly they have some recipe for growing a moustache unknown to the bulk of male Adelaide, judging by the finely-decorated upper lips I have seen on the box-seats of grubby-looking carriages.

Younger male Adelaide is intelligent—in many cases almost brilliant—but, hampered by ridiculous conventionalities, it rarely fulfils its early promise. A few have risen superior to their environments, and these have done the wisest thing possible—left Adelaide far behind, and gone to better places.

Some few men have made fortunes here, and these almost always—with pardonable ingratitude!—go elsewhere to spend their wealth.

You men of Adelaide—poor, narrow-minded fools most of you!—would that you could learn, before it is too late, what good things you are missing—would that you could realise that there may be some good in people (and places) who do not share your own prejudices.

From all of which sweeping statement I exempt two classes—the Post Office officials and the Railway employés. I have never received more kindly courtesy anywhere than from these departments here—(I refer chiefly to the heads of departments) and for their unfailing kindness and attention I thank them. These officials will always take precedence in my mind as the most valuable assets in Adelaide.

One thing more—if any remarks in the foregoing chapter have offended any of my few friends here, I would ask them to remember that, being friends, they are of necessity exceptions!

Chapter II

THE WOMEN

THE misfortune of the Adelaide women is that they were not born quadrupeds—they are a kind of mistake for cats, and only lack the outward and visible sign of the feline tribe. (Hard to be cat by nature and inclination, and be compelled to wear the guise of woman!) Moreover, they make one believe in the old Spanish tradition, that cats are descended from snakes. The outward semblance of the Adelaide female is intense respectability, and of course, in many cases, being homely to look upon, and exceeding badly clothed, she has no temptation to err from the paths of strict propriety. The poorer type is terrible to look upon, and the rich women make one wonder how they manage to spend so much money in clothing their nakedness, and with such disastrous results. Still, there are a few younger specimens who are passing fair, and if rescued in time, might ornament a brighter sphere. We see large possibilities in younger female Adelaide, and

A group of friendly women taking afternoon tea at a garden party in Adelaide, c. 1910. [SLSA PRG-280-1-13-448]

this saddens us, knowing as we do that, if timely rescue is not effected, these fair maids will grow up like the older generation, and find their main recreation in discussing the foibles of women—aye, and men too—who are outside, or beyond their sympathies, and who are, doubtless, infinitely superior to themselves.

I appeal to all large-hearted, intelligent men from the other States—from anywhere, provided you are clean, well-behaved, and, incidentally, possessed of your fair share of this world's goods—come and marry the fair daughters of Adelaide. There are many who are good to look upon, and quite intelligent, and with care it is not too late for them to develop into good wives and mothers, and, better still, broad-minded, enlightened, interesting women.

There is also a less objectionable type of femininity here—the harmless—but she is uninteresting, and therefore not to be forgiven. She is usually stupid by nature, and charitable

by inclination, the sort of person of whom one says, "She's a dear, good woman—so kind." She cannot be objectionable, because she has no deep feelings—she cannot be morally bad, because she has no strong passions—and she cannot be spiteful, because she is soon taught that, having few charms, she cannot hope to compete with those who have.

Feminine Adelaide has, as we hinted before, wild and terrible ideas of dress; every gown she wears is a sartorial crime, and bitter is her hatred and jealousy for any who exploit clothes better, or less offensive than her own. It follows that, with such limitations she, as a type, hates a broad, cultured, or enlightened woman. I have watched the fate of one or two splendid brainy women here, and have inwardly smiled—Bow to the conventions, O woman! if you would appear well in the eyes of Adelaide.

To sample local charity—in a family of my acquaintance, the cook, a girl of nineteen, previously respectable, went wrong. In any civilized community the mistress, recognising a valuable servant would have done what she could at the time, and taken her back when the trouble was over. But the lady in question simply dismissed her, thereby offering a further incentive to a young girl to go wrong.

It must be remembered, however, that the unfortunate girl of Adelaide gets few of the advantages of higher education, and is generally brought up in total ignorance of the serious things of life.

I know one family of four daughters, the eldest twenty-one, who have never been allowed to enter a theatre, although their father, a tolerably well-educated man, says he believes in a thorough education. When it was suggested to him that his daughters might see the "Midsummer Night's Dream," he was horrified. To be sure, these girls are motherless—a kind, sensible mother would surely understand that Shakespeare is a desirable branch of education.

Let us glance at local society. In a street I know, on one corner, Rags, a cheap but successful draper, has reared a red and white edifice. Opposite, the lady who once sold hats to fairer sisters in Melbourne, espoused to quite an important person, has wormed her way into the chosen few. Further up, an inferior edition of the share market assumes the pretensions of a Grand Duke.

Then we have Tobacco married to Alcohol, and, basking in the smiles of the very select—a quondam shepherd and a city waitress united in holy matrimony, and entertaining largely; a nurse also secured one of the matrimonial prizes. The daughter of a cocky farmer has snared a son of one of Adelaide's first families; a dentist's apprentice (daughter of a handsome barmaid) has caught another.

There are funnier cases than these, but I forbear to cite them—I have quoted enough to show how aristocratic is the society that sets so high a store on its smiles and favours.

Just outside the social pale one or two decently educated men have married *nymphes de pavées*, but these of course are carefully shunned by Adelaide's best and fairest.

Women of Adelaide—If I have down-trodden your pet virtues, or wounded your susceptibilities, or flown in the face of your dearest prejudices, during a boring existence among you, it has been with the best motives—with a desire to keep abreast of the times, and not to become embedded in musty conventionalities.

Chapter III
THE LESSER ANIMALS

I HAVE not devoted much time to the classification of these, but I believe that they comprise chiefly mosquitoes, cockroaches, flies, rats, and Lady Kitty.

PART III

GENERALITIES

Chapter I

MANNERS AND CUSTOMS

I AM inclined to agree with a certain prelate of some unfrequented islands, who said of the inhabitants, "Customs beastly, manners none."

The most characteristic custom of female Adelaide is church-going—any church committee, prayer meeting, or bazaar, will tear her away from domestic duties. Sometimes she persuades her male belongings to accompany her, but they seem not to appreciate this attention, and generally wander wearily to church with a woe-begone "Duty-compels-me" air.

The men have only two customs, common to them all. The first is a tendency to look too often on the wine that is red. Hotel-keeping is a profitable business here, where the "come and have a drink" formula is repeated at intervals of five minutes all day, and, frequently, nearly all night. Particularly on the share market is this habit apparent, where every

Churchgoers arriving at St. Peter's Cathedral, Adelaide. c. 1918.
[SLSA PRG-280-1-9-309]

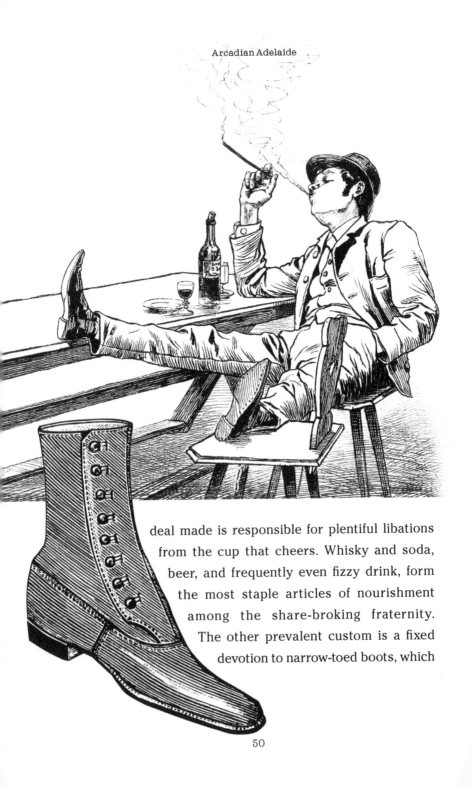

deal made is responsible for plentiful libations
from the cup that cheers. Whisky and soda,
beer, and frequently even fizzy drink, form
the most staple articles of nourishment
among the share-broking fraternity.
The other prevalent custom is a fixed
devotion to narrow-toed boots, which

common-sense and fashion (for once agreed) discarded long ago. The former habit is an evil, because far-reaching in hits results. In time it might kill its victims, but that would be a matter of small regret as many of them could well be spared. It is the misery said victims entail on their wives and mothers to which I take objection. The drinkers, having little intellect to destroy, do not lose much mentally by their Bacchanalian orgies, but they become vastly disagreeable to their fellow-creatures. Of the other custom—to wit, their taste in boots, there is little to be said, as it makes them uncomfortable, and does not hurt anyone else.

No comment that I could make would be severe enough to portray the utter brutishness of the villagers' manners—let the gentle reader go to the Mayor's ball, or any other public function, and judge for himself! When the supper rooms are thrown open, the guests fight like wild beasts, and their rush for food is like nothing I have ever seen so much as a pack of hungry beagles at feeling-time. Whether they fast for a week in order to avail themselves of these free repasts, I cannot say, but their greed is appalling.

The villagers' stare (this applies particularly to the female population) is an awful and shameless thing. Especially do they gaze at those of more pleasing appearance than themselves; whether from motives of scorn or of envy, I know not. The men do not, as a rule, indulge this habit—perhaps they are never sufficiently sober—but the women feast their eyes with undisguised rudeness on anything, female or otherwise, that interests them. To be sure the stare is not always so distressing as it is meant to be, because it is so difficult to take the villagers seriously. Scorn is wasted when emanating from an untidy female with a small intelligence and large feet, and it is difficult to be awe-inspiring in ready-made skirts and number six shoes! Moreover, said untidy females

have not sufficient tact or intelligence to conceal their evil feelings, and not enough courage to live up to them.

Monkshood says:—"An ugly woman, badly dressed is doubly damned—She is bad Nature and bad Art."

If that be true, female Adelaide in general is going fast to perdition.

Chapter II

INDUSTRIES

THE main industry of the Village is child-bearing, and Adelaide, both married and unmarried, does her best to help the birth-rate. Motherhood may be the noblest mission of women, but I question whether the Almighty Himself would approve of the perpetuation of some of the Village family-trees.

Fruit-growing is the local industry most deserving of praise, and must certainly qualify as a redeeming feature of the Village. Many of the successful growers are Chinamen. We may clamor for a White Australia, but it strikes one forcibly that the Yellow Mistake has helped materially to further national industries, especially fruit-growing.

But most of all, Adelaide prides herself on her wines. To pervert Scripture slightly—"We produce fruit, and children, and wine, but the greatest of these is Wine!" May a merciful God forgive Adelaide her wine, if He cannot find it in His heart to forgive the poor fools who drink it!

All the grapes on all the vines in all the vineyards of South Australia, helped by all the labor of all the employés of all the famous people who own those vines, could not produce one glass of wine to equal the *Vin Ordinaire* of France.

But has not the Almighty already shown His disapproval of this particular industry by burning down one of the most extensive cellars, with vats and vats of red wine, and white wine, and wine that isn't wine at all? *The Soil* grows the wine in France, and the French and Italians are born, as it were, to the art of wine-making. To import one or two skilled men is not enough—armies of them are required. Moreover, the wine is consumed as soon as it is made (this last fact is wonderful to anyone who has tasted it!), and it is one of the things which should be ancient. Had old Omar sampled Adelaide's wines, he would never have written—

"I often wonder what the vintners buy,
One half so precious as the stuff they sell."

The local vintners buy land, and houses, and household goods at, I suspect, the expense of many an unfortunate who has learned his first lessons in intemperance from their infernal concoctions—a cheap amusement certainly, but like most cheap things, nasty, and while getting beautifully into one's head, quite conducive to rheumatic gout. In fact, had Omar lived in Adelaide, he would never have sung the praises of the vine at all, his glorious "Rubaiyat" would not have been written, and the world would be the poorer for the loss. "Protect local industries!" Well and good, when the local manufactures are equal to the imported article; but, as in the case of wines, why put a prohibitive duty on what cannot be satisfactorily made in the State, thereby compelling the consumption by the masses of an inferior produce?

There are other local industries—some people have a sheep, and shear it once a year, some publish newspapers!—others breed horses (some of them good), others make inferior jam, and others again farm, with some profit.

But serious contemplation of the Great Wine Industry has ejected all minor ones from the writer's mind.

The wine matches the inhabitants, and I leave the reader to supply his own adjectives.

Chapter III

REDEEMING FEATURES

1. THE RAILWAY EMPLOYÉS
2. THE POST OFFICE OFFICIALS—
   Both of whom are deserving of the kindest memories,
   and of many other blessings.
3. THE CABMEN, who, as previously remarked, are quite
   efficient.
4. THE WHEAT (and indeed all cereals) is about as good as
   any in the World, and consequently,
5. THE FLOUR is excellent—it should certainly be exported
   to better places.
6. THE FRUIT is beyond reproach. In size, sweetness and
   flavour, it is the best in Australia, and rivals any in the
   world.
7. THE WEATHER, because it sometimes keeps the most
   disagreeable people indoors.
8. A RETURN TICKET TO MELBOURNE.

In conclusion, O "Arcadian Adelaide", may you improve—may your people prosper, and be happy, in order that they may remain in their own Village, and inflict themselves less on the outside world. May you some day awake to a sense of your own insignificance, and discover that the sun would shine, and the flowers bloom, and the birds sing on, even though you were sunk in the New Outer Harbor.

I wish you many good things, you people of Adelaide—but most of all I wish that you may soon be rid of my odious presence, which wish is probably mutual! And if these pages bear the imprint of many faults—if they anger, or—worse still—bore you, remember that there is no place on earth less calculated to foster literary merit than

ARCADIAN ADELAIDE.

THISTLE ANDERSON.

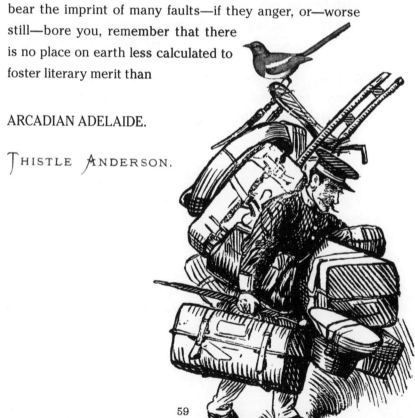

From

PRESS NOTICES OF THE DAY

Adelaide deserves all she gives it ... Thistle Anderson hits straight out, and the book is smartly, if venomously, written.
MELBOURNE TABLE TALK

Adelaide people and their ways are cuttingly satirised ... Whether one agrees with the writer's conclusions or not, the book is admittedly clever and pungent. BARRIER MINER

The book of the hour is Arcadian Adelaide *... It is cleverly written, and it 'booms'.* MELBOURNE PUNCH

Thistle Anderson takes a subject in hand in a direct hit-out-from-the-shoulder manner, with a sledge-hammer like force that is refreshing in this age of sophistry. ADELAIDE WEEKLY NEWS

Her book Arcadian Adelaide, *is selling like hot cakes, and the early editions are sold out ... Cleverly written, and in some chapters a delicate—in print—subject is dealt with in a way that can be read by the most fastidious ...* ADELAIDE TRUTH

A Marie Corelli in the midst of us ... The book indicates a brilliant mind ...   QUIZ

She is the woman of the hour ... She little dreamed she would wake up to find herself famous. Her book has unearthed many imitators, but there is only one Thistle Anderson.
                                                ADELAIDE TRUTH

Thistle Anderson's second book, The Arcadians, *has been eagerly sought after, and has further enhanced the author's reputation as a clever and talented pen-pusher.*
                                                ADELAIDE TRUTH

The Arcadians ... *intensely feminine, and decidedly witty ... made a big hit ...*   STEELE RUDD'S MAGAZINE

Our only comment on the book is that we are sorry for Miss Anderson.   ADELAIDE ADVERTISER

Arcadian Adelaide *is forty pages of stabs with forty poisoned hat pins.*   BULLETIN

Arcadian Adelaide *has had the effect of waking Adelaide up with such a shock, the like of which has never been known before.*   'Milly' QUIZ

A little knowledge is a dangerous thing, more especially in a woman.   QUIZ

And from John Norton's scurrilous reply in the Melbourne *Truth:*

The picture of the authoress, Thistle, appears on the first page ... It does not match the thistle on the cover. It is toothy and flabby, and shabby in lineal, suggestive of a big hand and a splay foot, and a naturally bad temper, worsened by sought after nasty experiences, and consequent disappointment ... First question which occurs to any sane person ... What has happened to her? What extraordinary thing has she tried to do in Adelaide, and how has she come to fall in?

What did they say to you in Adelaide, Thistle, or what did they fail to do? What was your estimate of yourself, and what was their estimate of you? Did you want an aide de camp for a toy, or a fat and unsuspecting silver king for a hubby? Did you thrash the social waters pretty hard with all sorts of flies for the one and the other, and did each one regard you with a mild curiosity and glide along to more attractive metal? It seems so, indeed, poor Thistle ...

You have found out a lot about boarding houses, Thistle, and just here it seems opportune to observe that we might have a good deal smarter and more readable booklet if those boardinghouse-keepers and others would put together all that they found out about you.

It is not for one moment to be assumed that it would be naughty enough to be really interesting, for your style and your matter smack very much more of weak imaginings and unfulfilled desires than of the riot and rapture of fierce full life ...

Still there is a bit of hope for you (and for Adelaide) in that you have got a husband. You saved one soul out of the unspeakable city. And let us hope that in time he may save yours. The main industry of the village, you say, is child-bearing. Well, get to it. The children of your body may do you more credit than the offspring of your mind ... *Quit books for babies.*

Victoria Park racecourse in the 1890s. Height of fashion!
Adelaide City Archives HP0095

Arcadian
Adelaide.

CHLOROFORM

THISTLE ANDERSON

in

EDWARDIAN ADELAIDE

DEREK WHITELOCK

THE SCENE

THE year 1905 saw the Russo-Japanese war raging, the fall of
Port Arthur and the sinking of a big Russian fleet, in an hour
or so, by the Japanese in the Tsushima Straits. There was a
revolution in Russia and Bloody Sunday on the streets of St
Petersburg. There was a crisis in Morocco. Albert Einstein
published his Theory of Relativity.

But Adelaide seemed quiet.

For Edwardian Adelaide this was par for the course.
The only occurrence the *Yearbook of South Australia* deems
worthy of recording for 1905 in its 'Principal Events' was that
the first kindergarten in South Australia was opened. This is
sinister censorship, for in fact Adelaide was deeply stirred.
The *Yearbook*'s compilers might well have noted that the year
also witnessed a pretty storm in the Adelaide teacup with
the publication in April, by a reckless Twin Street publisher,
of Thistle Anderson's *Arcadian Adelaide*. Such was the civic

shock over this little red pamphlet with a thistle on its cover that it ran through ten editions in 1905. A sequel called *The Arcadians* went through four editions. Thistle delightedly called herself 'the Transgressor' and dedicate *The Arcadians* to any readers who, deserving mention, were unintentionally omitted from *Arcadian Adelaide*'s pages.

Arcadian Adelaide was a thistle under the municipal bottom. It stirred up a furore in the press. At the end of a column and a half of quotation and abuse, the *Advertiser* concluded: 'Our only comment on the book is that we are sorry for Miss Anderson'. John Norton, the infamous Melbourne *Truth* journalist, published a special broadsheet *Reply* to say that *Arcadian Adelaide* wasn't worth notice. His advice to Thistle was to 'quit books for babies'.

A Mrs F. Ellis was moved to write, and pay for, a pamphlet in response called *A Scratch from an Adelaide 'Cat'*. (Thistle had said that some Adelaide women were cats.) In this, among much else, Mrs Ellis perpetrated the following stanzas:

You say you've been crushed by this village so holy,
No doubt by the celluloid-collared men so lowly;
And yet to be crushed by these men do we think jolly,
Do we 'cats'.

In conclusion, dear Thistle, this is no place for you,
And we'll tell you just the best thing you can do—
Go back to heaven! We wish you adieu.
Do we 'cats'.

The *Bulletin* considered *Arcadian Adelaide* to be 'forty pages of stabs with forty poisoned hat pins'. Imagination boggles at what the Adelaide City Council thought of it. In *The Arcadians* Thistle reveals that she received many anonymous letters, 'to the extent of a thousand', mostly hostile.

Many … bleats have come in from the poor, dear Village lambs (who will probably prove goats on Judgement Day, and be relegated to the left of the Lord), but to me the most interesting part of the book—labour rewarded, as it were—is the fact that so many that sit in high places, while outwardly and officially condemning the book and the author, have given ample manifestation … that in secret they gloat over it … One lofty power, who is also a slight Bacchanalian, and who serves South Australia for £1,000 per annum, said, 'Of course I am tied up with leagues of red tape, and I dare not get up on the roof and proclaim my opinion—but privately, I agree with every word in the book'.

The pamphlet's success shows that many of its arrows thudded into their targets and that several readers enjoyed seeing the city's famous self-satisfaction pierced. Thistle obviously relished the controversy. 'A kind notice sells one book,' she reflects, 'where a scurrilous one sells a hundred, and I court criticism—The bitterer, the better I like it.'

Why all the fuss? And who was this handsome Mrs Herbert Fisher of the impeccable North Adelaide address, who chose to call herself Thistle Anderson and lambaste the City of Churches with trenchant prose?

THE CITY

ADELAIDE had good reason to be proud of itself in 1905. Founded in 1836 by 'systematic colonizers' following the precepts of the outstanding theoretician Edward Gibbon Wakefield, Adelaide was the principal city of a province – *not* a colony of England – and had always been conscious of the fact that she was different from (most citizens would have said better than) other enclaves of the Empire. Holdfast Bay was never allowed to become another Botany Bay with its chain gangs, soldiery and sin. South Australia developed along generally admired lines of planned development and settlement, with assisted and selected immigration. With its backdrop of hills, broad encompassing parklands and handsome buildings, Adelaide was a superb, planned city, thanks to the foresight of Colonel William Light.

Most South Australians lived far more comfortably and spaciously, in well-built villas and cottages with fruitful gardens, than they would have done in Britain or Ireland. Adelaide was noted for its churches, temperance societies, insurance companies, banks, brass bands, gardens and thrusting business houses such as Elders and John Martins. It was progressive: the first Australian city to achieve local government, install deep drainage, and give the vote, in 1894, to women. Eminent visitors like Mark Twain, who thought Adelaide 'a paradise for the working man', Anthony Trollope, who especially liked the Botanic Gardens and the General Post Office building, and Price Alfred, Duke of Edinburgh, who observed in 1867 that Adelaide had fewer of 'the poor and rowdy class' conspicuous in other Australian cities, enthused over such features.

And Adelaide was strong on respectability. The founding fathers were vehement on this. 'If I can get pious people sent out to that land,' declared George Fife Angus, 'the ground will be blessed for their sake.' Pious people, stern proponents of the Protestant ethic, were sent or attracted to South Australia in many thousands. To an extraordinary degree South Australians were Nonconformists or evangelical Anglicans. As advocates of the Victorian virtues of self help, thrift, conspicuous morality, political reform and sabbatarianism, they worked to make Adelaide a model city. Geographically isolated and a bit introspective, Adelaideans cherished their sense of difference. They published books and made speeches proclaiming this with pride. Turn-of-the century Adelaide was the conscious apotheosis of Victorian respectability.

'Respectable' racegoers at Victoria Park racecourse, Adelaide. Theodore Bruce, South Australian auctioneer and politician is standing third from the left, 1907. [SLSA PRG 280/1/11/561]

THISTLE ANDERSON

THEN along came Thistle Anderson with her blistering little book. She called their proud, planned city a Village, and the respectable ratepayers Villagers. She claimed that there were more opium dens and prostitutes in 'Holy Adelaide' than in wicked Melbourne, a city three times bigger. Far from being a bastion of teetotalism, Adelaide was remarkable for drunks. There was only one theatre, and one decent hotel, the incomparable South Australian, demolished, sadly, in 1972. Adelaide men were boors in narrow-toed boots; Adelaide women 'passing plain to look upon', and badly dressed. They were narrow-minded, 'and their cardinal virtues ... Religious Belief and Conventionality'. She called their religion 'Churchianity'. They were snobbish, hypocritical, and even cruel to horses, especially the horses pulling the trams. (Thistle recommended that the tram owners should be 'boiled to slow music'.) 'May a merciful God,' she prayed, 'forgive Adelaide her wine.' 'The main industry ... is child-bearing ... but I question whether the Almighty Himself would approve of the perpetuation of some of the Village family-trees.' Her unkindest cut was the remark that the best thing about Adelaide was that you could buy a ticket to Melbourne at the railway station.

And so it went on. But who was this immigrant harpy, ignorant of Light's vision and dismissive of all Torrens-side progress?

Well, it would have grieved Mrs Ellis and John Norton, but Mrs Herbert Fisher was a lady of character, style and note. She rates detailed mention in E. Morris Miller's bibliography *Australian Literature*, and nearly two pages in Paul Depasquale's admirable *Critical Study of South Australian Literature*. Leonard Henslowe's 'A Chat with Thistle Anderson' published in *Henslowe's Annual* for 1903 reveals her as a beautiful and well-educated Scotswoman, of Kiplingesque imperial beliefs, much travelled, who confessed to two years on the stage and a love for adventure and vigorous outdoor life. Her publications, favourably reviewed in the British press, include short stories, *Dives' Wife and Other Fragments* (A. Gardner, Paisley, Scotland, 1908), and books of verse such as *Verses at Random* (A. Gardner, 1902) and *Songs to Dorian and Other Verses* (J. Long, London, 1901). (The first two can be read in the South Australian State Library's Reference Section and the South Australian Collection.)

Thistle Anderson's verse is a bit florid, typical of its time, but fiery and romantic. It also tells us much about the writer. For example, the poem 'Derelict' in *The Reveller, and Vagabond Verses* (published in Adelaide by Vardon and Pritchard in 1905, presumably on the crest of *Arcadian Adelaide's* commercial success) reveals her as a passionate woman, and a great traveller:

Oh! Those merry days in 'Frisco,
Or those larks in sunny France,
And the hours that sped so swiftly,
Bright with music, song and dance.

I have fished the Highland waters,
Shot the heather-sprinkled moors,
Climbed Mount Arthur's Seat—O! Scotland
Home! You call with tempting lures.

I have felt the snows of Russia,
And the throbbing Indian heat—
Seen the midnight sun in Norway,
Stemmed her fjiords with tireless feet.

But those feet were tiring, and after further adventures in 'the islands of the South', 'age creeps on' over the Derelict and she heads for Australia, about which she has some startling expectations:

I have come to you, Australia!
Like a tired child sinks to rest.
In your wooded hills are buried
Hopes once cherished in my breast.

Land of lonely deaths and fancies,
Where each insect has a sting—
Where the tropic flow'rs are scentless,
And the songbirds never sing . . .

Let my body, face to skyward,
Bleach upon your trackless plains—
Let the hungry dingo, seeking,
Draw the cold blood from my veins.

Thistle was clearly a goer. In 'The Reveller' she expresses other un-Adelaidean sentiments:

Hurrah! For a body made for Love,
Voluptuous, soft and fair,
Aquiver with passion and hot desire—
With mantle of dusky hair—
With arms that languish for close caress
In the solemn hush of night,
Blue eyes that shine thro' the shadows dim
With a tender passion-light ...
Red wine, fair women and summer skies,
Who cares what the grey-beards say?

For 1905 this was strong stuff; scandalous for Adelaide! Summer skies, certainly; red wine, perhaps, in moderation and with the curtains drawn. But fair women emitting passion-light? The grey-beards would have been speechless. But as loyal subjects they would have agreed with the other Thistle Anderson revealed in 'To the King':

'Long live the King!' ring out ye bells, ring out
Your merry peals, and let the trumpets sound
The joyous tidings, quelling fear and doubt,
We thank Thee, Lord, our well-lov'd King is crown'd.
From India and from Afric', hand in hand,
Men who have fought for England meet once more
As loyal subjects of the Motherland.

There was a great deal more in this vein. The poem had been commissioned by the respectable London journal *Hearth and Home* and was published in their coronation issue in 1902.

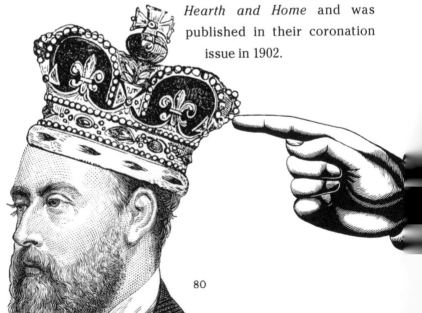

MRS FISHER

SUCH glimpses of Thistle were all we had until recently, when [historian] Pat Stretton did some biographical sleuthing, for which I am most grateful. She pursued Thistle's pricklings through the public records and Town Hall archives, and the yellowing gossip columns of the vanished Adelaide journals, *Quiz*, *Critic* and *Observer*.

Thistle was the daughter of George Anderson. He was well-educated, well-off and fond of writing verse, and was Liberal Member of Parliament for Glasgow from 1868 to 1885. In March of that year he came to Australia as Deputy Master of the Mint in Melbourne. The *Sydney Bulletin* later (11 August 1900) reported that this 'elderly verse-writing politician' had

> married a 17-year-old Scotch beauty, then Miss Pollie Clowering, now an ample but attractive lady, in appearance not much older than her own daughter. The latter, while her father lived, was a pupil in a convent. But the death of the

white-bearded theorist changed matters. His widow was soon engaged to be married and his daughter grabbed the desire of her heart and entered the Ballet.

Described as 'a big blonde, buxom girl', Thistle presently joined the touring company of Nance O'Neil, an American actress specializing in tragic roles like Camille and Lady Macbeth. J.C. Williamson brought the company to Adelaide in 1900, and Thistle appeared as the Baroness in *Fedora*. The *Bulletin* observed that her 'shy histrionic demeanour comes as a surprise to acquaintances who, in real life, don't find her timid'. Thistle travelled with the company throughout Australia, to New Zealand, and then to London. There in December 1901 she married Herbert Fisher, a thirty-five-year-old Adelaide stockbroker, son of a rich grain merchant.

In the *Critic* through 1902 and 1903 the gossip columnist 'Lady Kitty' kept South Australia informed of the Fishers' conspicuous lifestyle in the Old Country. They lived in London for a while, and Thistle was presented at Court. Wistful Adelaide socialites read that

> Mrs Herbert Fisher ... who, in Australia dabbled in journalism and aspired to the stage, has published a book of verses, which has made a hit ... Since her marriage, Mrs Fisher has abandoned Bohemia, revels in big, feathery hats and Worth gowns, and goes everywhere. The Countess of Maimi ... is presenting her at Court.

never hav... seen a...thing so ha.. in Australia.

Bits of t...atrical g...p sifted from..y London ...ts tell ... people we ... known in ...tralia. ... Conway Tead.. who was o.. here wi... the ill-fated ... Hur co., i... playing ...rincipal part... The best of Friends, ...orgeous prod...tion at Dr..y-lane; it ends at 7.30 a... ends at 11.0. The ...ter says Ria Holt does ... Drury-l... pieces quite magnificent... considere... the differen.. in size of stages. Drur... he has an enor...mous stage. Mrs. Ma...re Morris has a small part in Chance ...Idol at Wynd...ham's Theatre. She ...ears beautiful clothes, but hasn't muc... o say. George Titheradge is also in th... cast. He hasn't much of a par... doesn't suit him, but he is always ...tistic. King Hedley has a very sma... art in Secret and Confidential at the ...medy Theatre. Percy Brough is in the ...ast also, and plays a small detective p...

The great Dolores give... her first con...cert in the Town Hall to...orrow (Thurs...day). After phenomenal triumphs in the other States, those Adelaideans who had not heard her before are anxious to do so, and the booking has been splendid. At her last concert in Melbourne hun...dreds were turned away from the door, and had it been possible to sell them niches in the wall and Corinthian columns would have brought big prices. Many people tried to persuade her busi...ness managers that it was madness to appear in Melbourne on the same night as Melba. But on that occasion their croaking was belied by the fact that Dolores had a bigger house than Melba.

At Dolores' Melbourne Concerts she was deluged with floral tributes, and each night a procession of flower bearers, com...posed of managers and ushers, followed her to her carriage, but by the time they reached the footpath all that was left of the bouquets were pieces of silver paper which encased the stems. The enthusias...tic crowds rushed her flowers for memen...toes of the sweet songbird, and not only women, but crowds of men eagerly grab...bed a blossom to keep in memory of her sweet notes.

It is absolutely ridiculous to notice the amount of disapprobation bestowed on Dolores concert gowns now that she is making such triumphs. In the old days, when she was just the same glorious sin...ger, appreciated only by the cultured and artistic few, those gowns were good enough for us. Nobody objected to them then. The Frenchy attire of la Melba has evidently inspired misguided jour...nalists to imbue Dolores with fashion journal ideas. Dolores does not require to be tricked out in "smart" dressing. She can stand alone—simply natural, without a trace of makeup of any kind. Besides, so-called "fashionable" clothes would not suit her, and that finishes it.

LADY KITTY.

A London correspondent writes: "When Anglo-Australia was operating in Brisols tin shares a few months ago for a substantial rise, Aimée Moore, formerly a well-known amateur actress in Mel...ourne, became a "bear" of two thousand shares at a guinea on the usual deposit ...rms. She has just closed the account ...ith the shares at 15/ each, and now miles at the "bulls.""

Mrs. Brown-Potter has disposed of her ...wo London houses, Burleigh Lodge and ..., Abbey-road, both in St. John's Wood, ...ad has purchased further property at ...aldenhead, where her river residence, ...ray Lodge, remains one of the prettiest ...uses on the lovely Thames reach. She ...as an immense fruit and vegetable gar...n, and keeps six ponies. Her mother is present a guest at Bray Lodge.

J. Thomson photo. Bedford.
Mrs. Herbert Fisher.

Percy Grainger is doing remarkably well on the Patti tour, and the diva is among those who say that the young Vic...torian knows much that he can never have been taught in this world. Those who have heard this boy discourse on art, lite...rature, philosophy, and science hold that he must be inspired. In addition, young Grainger is remarkably handsome.

Ada Crossley goes to America next year. Whenever she does visit Australia, she means to keep her old promise and sing at St. Mary's R.C. Cathedral in Syd...ney and the Australian Church in Mel...bourne, where she formerly sang in the choir without much thought of European fame or fortune. Her success at the Norwich Festival last week (October 20-25) was phenomenal. Old Signor Ran...degger took both her hands and kissed them after the Brahms Rhapsody, over which The Times gave her one of the most eulogistic criticisms that has ever appeared in its columns. A. C. has quite a remarkable instinct for German music.

Agnes G. Murphy means to revisit Melbourne at the close of the next Lon...don season. She will then have been eight years in London. On her arrival she was taken up warmly by her old friend, Amy Sherwin, whose husband was then managing Paderewski, and in this way she got to know all the best musical people. Miss Murphy has naturally de...veloped and improved her opportunities since then, and was lately described by the editor of the Musical Herald as "the best informed journalist in London on musical matters generally."

A full page of Miss Alice Crawford's pictures, with attractive letterpress, ap...peared in a recent number of the Sport...ing and Dramatic News.

A remarkable instance of the value of a name is demonstrated in the change in Madame Minna Fischer's position since leaving Australia Minna Fischer put in a long period of hard study with Stock...hausen at Frankfort, who is believed by many to be the greatest living teacher of singing. Then Minna Fischer tried her luck in London, and for a long time had a very hard experience, but eventually things began to brighten, and she secur...ed a fair number of pupils at 7/6 a lesson. Less than two years ago she was brought under the notice of Melba, who, after hearing her give lessons and satisfying herself by other trying means, declared Madame Fischer to be a teacher of quite remarkable gifts. The use of Melba's name—gracefully volunteered by the great singer—acted like magic, and where formerly it was a struggle to get pupils at a crown and a half a lesson, she cannot now give appointments to all who are ready with a guinea for a sharp half hour.

Arthur Streeton's striking picture of Trafalgar-square, the "Heart of the Empire," is on all sides admitted to be the finest work he has ever done. Hopes are entertained among his fellow artists that it may find a place in the National Gallery of his native State—Victoria. Longstaff, Mackennal, Allston, Bunny, and Phil May say it is a work of extra...

ordinary brilliancy. A fair copy of it was awarded "honorable mention" at this year's Paris Salon.

Mr. George Clutsam has been seriously ill, but when the mail left was improving. Mr. Kennerley Rumford, husband of Clara Butt, made a great hit at the Norwich Festival with two of Clutsam's songs, which were by no means the best work of this clever composer, who has to write down to the popular taste as a rule.

Miss Annie Sabine leaves for England in March.

Mr. Hugh Corbin returned to Adelaide on Saturday.

Mrs. Alfred Astley has returned from Melbourne.

Mr. R. Barr Smith is building a house in Angas-street.

Mr. and Mrs. R. Barr Smith are in South Yarra, Vic.

Miss A. Stirling leaves for England early in the new year.

Mrs. C. Parry arrived on a visit to Adelaide last Wednesday.

Mrs. Smithson Dunn will not be At Home till May 3, 1903.

Mr. Jack Downer arrived from Albany on Thursday for a holiday.

Dr. and Mrs. E. A. Johnson leave for London on Thursday, December 11.

Mr. and Mrs. Wybert Reeve are tho...roughly enjoying London. Miss Meta Büring is with them.

Mr. and Mrs. E. C. Clucas and Master Clucas leave shortly on a trip to Tas...mania and New Zealand.

The many friends of Mrs. Cawley, who is at present in London, will be sorry to hear she has been suffering from ill-health.

Mrs. E. W. Way leaves on Thursday for England. Miss M. Way will accom...pany her as far as Western Australia, where she will be married shortly after her arrival.

Mr., Mrs. R. Barr Smith have been staying for the last month at Mrs. Lowen's comfortable hotel at Woodside en route for Melbourne, where they will spend the summer.

Lady Way gave a small garden party at Government House on Tuesday after...noon to give the friends of Miss Marion Way the opportunity of saying good-bye to her before leaving for the West.

They're telling a very funny story in Broken Hill about the bride and bride...groom who, after the ceremony and its attendant festivities, on reaching home found all the doors fastened up and the keyholes blocked with putty, and had to enter through a window. Indoors, too, candles and kerosine had mysteriously disappeared, and the gas service had also been rendered ineffective. But the groom had a few matches left.

A very successful juvenile dance was given in the Strathalbyn Institute on Friday evening by the pupils of Mrs. Cameron's (of Mount Barker) class. It was the wind up of the season, and Mrs. Cameron is to be congratulated on the efficiency of her scholars. Miss Smyth supplied the music, and amongst those present were Mrs. Cameron, and Miss Olive Cameron, Misses Lempriere, Rich...ardson, Taylor, Cheriton, Crowder, Rogers (2), Tucker, Phillips (2), Hender...son, and Adams, Masters Tucker, Butler (2), Taylor (3), and Lempriere.

Socially Broken Hill has been very dull lately. A Jewish wedding, Mr. Israel Krantz to Miss Sophie Warschaw...skey, was of interest to the chosen. The ceremony was performed by the Rev. A. T. Boas, of Adelaide, and was followed by a ball and supper, attended by about fifty guests. The Quartette Club last

'Lady Kitty' of the *Critic* and 'Milly' of *Quiz* were the reigning gossip queens of Adelaide. To read their columns is to enter a lost, stagnant world of snobbery, sycophancy and genteel malice. Lady Kitty (whose *nom-de-plume* lingered on in the *Advertiser* until the 1940s), soon fell foul of Thistle – among the 'lesser animals' listed in *Arcadian Adelaide* we find 'mosquitoes, cockroaches, flies, rats, and Lady Kitty'.

The Fishers returned to Adelaide in 1903. They stayed at the South Australian Hotel for a month, visited Melbourne, then rented 'Stramshall' at 150 Hill Street, North Adelaide. A commodious gentleman's residence built in 1902, it [was] still in excellent order in 1984. While Herbert was sharebroking, Thistle moved through Adelaide society. In November 1904 'Milly' wrote in *Quiz* about Thistle at the Children's Hospital Fete:

> Mrs Herbert Fisher was unique in her early Victorian costume which looked lovely, but not nearly so striking as the heliotrope costume she wore just lately. I hear she has written a book on Adelaide, and I must certainly get a copy, as it will no doubt be good reading.

In April 1905 *Arcadian Adelaide* appeared. It was roasted by the *Advertiser*. Thistle wrote to the paper complaining about the severity of the review.

> I reiterate what I have already stated in my preface—that the book is intended merely as a playful skit, and that there is no malice in it—only an irresistible love of the lighter side of things and a desire to extract amusement from everything.

Her plea strikes one as perhaps disingenuous in the light of her other remarks about 'courting criticism'.

The reviewer in *Quiz* of 5 May 1905 was also hostile, concluding: 'All that *Quiz* can say on the production is that "a little knowledge is a dangerous thing", more especially in a woman.' But 'Milly' in the same issue was loyal to Thistle. Gossiping about the Victoria Park races, she wrote:

> I'm sorry Mrs Herbert Fisher was not there to hear herself and her book discussed ... She would have thoroughly enjoyed it ... Though there are many things in the book which may not be palatable to some of the community, still there is a large substratum of truth in what she writes. And it has had the effect of waking Adelaide up with such a shock, the like of which has never been known before. Mrs Fisher is a thorough cosmopolitan, having seen much of the world, and therefore is competent to take a broader view than most of the inhabitants of the Arcadian city.

The Fishers left Adelaide about the middle of 1905 and went, after some time in Melbourne and San Francisco, back to London. Little is known of Thistle after that. Herbert died in 1912. The *Critic*'s obituary reported that his widow 'was enjoying life in Paris when last heard of'.

SOME COMMENTS

THISTLE'S tart comments on Adelaide and its inhabitants can be judged by the reader, but as the comments were made on a long-gone scene some background information may help. That the city outwardly professed, even by the British standards of the time, puritanical conventions, and that many found these stifling, cannot be doubted. Adelaide society was essentially White Anglo-Saxon Protestantism on parade, and proud of it. Douglas Pike in his *Paradise of Dissent* wrote of Adelaide's 'nobly depressing rectitude'.

But it was the isolated little city's collective smugness and hypocrisy about unadmitted social problems which irritated some visitors, and infuriated Thistle. A correspondent to the *Sydney Morning Herald* in 1907 wrote: 'As I entered Adelaide a gentleman in the train said to me with a wave of his hand: "My dear sir, the finest city on earth, and I have travelled a good deal".' 'You are proud,' Caroline Chisholm wrote to the

Register in 1849, 'and have reason to be, of your city, but I am almost weary of this Adelaide, Adelaide ...'

R.E.N. Twopenny in his *Town Life in Australia* (1883) thought South Australia's morality made it 'the New England of the Antipodes'. He continued:

In Adelaide middle class respectability is too strong for larrikinism, and reports a far healthier moral tone than obtains in either Melbourne or Sydney; but for these advantages the little town pays the small but disagreeable price of Philistinism. Want of culture, Phariseeism and narrow mindedness find a more congenial home there than anywhere else in Australia ...

Snobbery was rife, too, although the local press, which even Thistle admits was lively, was not slow to detect and ridicule it. For instance, when in 1849 John Morphett proposed that South Australians prominent in the Land Sales Book should get hereditary titles, the *Register* thought the notion 'fudge in its purest absurdity', the idea of 'an indifferently-shingled legislator'.

There is no doubt, too, that the sabbatarianism noted by Thistle was excessive in Adelaide – it remained so well into living memory. The old Adelaide Sunday meant black, sweltering clothes, bone-numbing pews, padlocks on the children's playgrounds, solemn disposition, no beer – even the trains were kept to a moral minimum. The wowsers banned swimming on Glenelg's beaches for many years, and even when it was permitted the sexes had to disport themselves in separate cages on either side of the jetty.

Just as conspicuous and influential as the sabbatarians were the temperance enthusiasts, especially those 'God's Police', the hyperactive White Ribboners of the Woman's Christian Temperance Union. Old photographs of these

Group holding a sign in the shape of a cross saying 'Yes Jesus died for you poor sinner' reading from the bottom to the top. Believed to be either the Band of Hope or Christian Endeavour. c. 1921. [SLSA B-68803]

gimlet-eyed, funereal zealots, many of them in widow's caps and clutching placards, lend support to Thistle's contention that 'the Adelaide female ... in many cases, being homely to look upon, and exceedingly badly clothed ... has no temptation to err from the paths of strict propriety'. The White Ribboners, singing 'Hold High the Torch', formed a shieldwall of starch against the Devil, especially as made manifest in bottled beer. They lobbied brilliantly for women's suffrage, then used their new electoral power to hound the drinkers and gamblers through the legislature. They were prominent in achieving the restrictive Licensing Act of 1908; but their chief glory was their successful push for six o'clock closing, with the notorious 'Six O'Clock Swill' which debased Adelaide's drinking from 1915 until the 1960s.

To be fair, the Union was equally active in its campaign against opium dens and prostitution. Thistle was right to criticize 'the Queen City of the South' for its broad and unadmitted seamy side. As early as 1842 a petition had been presented to Governor Gawler objecting to 'the large number of females who are living a life of prostitution in the City ... out of proportion to the respectable population'. Nor is it doubted that Adelaide liked the bottle. As early as 1837 Judge Jeffcott complained about 'the alarming extent of the vice of drunkenness' in Adelaide. In 1853 a young immigrant, C.H. Barton, wandered 'the queer, dusty town' and complained in a letter to his sister that 'there were far too many taverns' occupied by 'sharp company in white Panama hats' who drank brandy nobblers and raspberry spiders. There was a pub every few yards down many of the streets, open until all hours before the temperance forces got at them. Many Adelaideans were frequently and publicly drunk, and ladies, often signing themselves 'Disgusted', complained in the press about bad language and 'blackguards who have been known to insult young ladies who happen to be alone'.

Poster for the Referendum on temperance and the six o'clock closing, 1916. Photographer: William Charles Brooker. SLSA PRG 1316/16/15

Readers can judge Thistle's comments on Adelaide's weather, hills and buildings themselves. Here I think she is talking through her feathered hat.

It is startling to be reminded that in 1905 Adelaide had only one active theatre – the exquisite Theatre Royal, which opened in 1868 – and one music hall. Local theatres had been lively in colonial times, as had other arts and entertainments. They have been so again, in a tradition of which the Festival is a natural development. But the Edwardian years were strangely short of high culture.

That hiatus did not deter Mrs Ellis, who endeavoured to put 'poor, wee Thistle' right in her incredible *Scratch from an Adelaide 'Cat'*. (There were at least three other anti-Thistle pamphlets even worse than that one. One argued that Adelaide was not dull: it had a skating rink.) As we read Mrs Ellis we begin to understand why *Arcadian Adelaide* was written.

> She says we 'have only one theatre and that one is only poorly patronized'. This surely speaks well for the sociabilities of Adelaide people. They are more homely, and entertain in a more friendly way amongst themselves than in any other part of Australia. There are not sufficient of the outcast class in Adelaide, for which we are truly grateful. We are more hospitable, more liberal-minded, more homely in every way, and home is home to us. When we can derive vast pleasure from our friendly home gatherings what do we want with more theatres?

Thistle obviously got around the pubs, which caused Mrs Ellis to clack her dentures: 'Oh! Thistle, Thistle, how do you know all these things about liquor? ... I cannot say from personal tasting whether the liquors sold are good or bad, but when Hubby sometimes comes home after having sampled a few he seems to think that they are all right.'

Thistle's description of the grand old South Australian Hotel as 'a veritable oasis in the desert' may displease male readers. John Norton drew attention at the time to the old York (since demolished) and the Botanic; and pubs like the Stag, the Austral, the Rob Roy, the North Adelaide, the Queen's Head, the Producers and many others were and are hospitable places – but perhaps not to lady drinkers in 1905; women were barred from most of their bars until the 1970s.

Thistle had little praise to dispense in *Arcadian Adelaide,* though she did mention a few things in passing. In *The Arcadians* she added to her brief list of good things the locally grown tobacco, butter, the *Register* and the *Advertiser,* albeit they were 'too hidebound by conventional prejudices', and the cocoa dispensed at the Crown and Anchor inn. She also confessed to some pleasant memories of the countryside:

> ... those glorious drives through hills made beautiful by glistening rain or autumnal sunshine—those morning gallops over crisp seaweed and silver sand, alone with Nature, revelling in the strange mute sympathy between horse and rider. She will picture the misty moonlight on the beach at Glenelg, the crimson splendour of mountain sun-sets, enjoyed with well-loved dogs and horses ...

Maybe Thistle enjoyed a drive in a Tourist Bureau charabanc at Mount Lofty in the Adelaide Hills, but maybe not the 'company'.
[SLSA PRG-280-1-26-133]

CONCLUSIONS

WITHOUT a doubt *Arcadian Adelaide* drew blood. Ten editions (or more correctly impressions) and massive press and private comment signify that the little red pamphlet was the literary event of the year. Thistle devoted two chapters of *The Arcadians* to her critics and letter writers. She referred to long reviews, occasionally favourable but usually abusive, in journals as diverse as the *Critic*, the *Standard,* the *Barrier Mines* ('unexpected in its kindness'), *Punch, Quiz* and *Tocsin.* She devoted another chapter to *A Scratch from an Adelaide 'Cat'*, returning libel for libel, but Mrs Ellis's 'downright, exceedingly personal drivel' is not in her league. To belie Thistle's picture of the Adelaide male, Mrs Ellis had printed a portrait of her own husband with a caption parodying Thistle's style – 'one of Adelaide's celluloid-collared, narrow-toed booted, shallow-brained fools'. 'Just for once,' hissed Thistle, 'we agree with her—he looks it.' Then she turned to Mrs Ellis's syntax:

> We quote one sentence verbatim, punctuation and all—'Not only this, but there are some and a real good percentage of superior and highly-cultured and refined girls and women in Adelaide where in good looks and superiority you, Thistle, whose main attribute seems to be brass, are not fit to wipe the feet of.' The composition of that sentence would make the Gods weep.

She rightly ignored John Norton's *Reply* as 'personal slander rather than a critique'.

Why did Thistle do it? Paul Depasquale thinks that something about Adelaide had upset her, so she dashed off the pamphlet as a joke and was startled by the solemn reaction. I doubt this. I think that Thistle, enraged by the city's 'musty conventionality', hit where she knew it would hurt most. She sneered at Adelaide morality, institutions, style, culture and the appearance of the citizens – she was leading with the chin. (More recently, Festival Director Christopher Hunt elicited similar strong reaction when he called Adelaide dull and her womenfolk dowdy.) I suspect Thistle revelled in the notoriety and the vilification heaped upon *Arcadian Adelaide* and its author. And she sold lots of books.

Why pick on sheltered Adelaide, when all Victorian/ Edwardian English-speaking cities from Manchester to Melbourne were stifled by the same blanket of conventional morality? Probably just because that is where Thistle found herself, and because Adelaide was so excessively proud of its 'self-constituted halo'.

Hugh Stretton remarks in his *Ideas for Australian Cities*:

It was easy to mock the respectable society of the old Adelaide oligarchy. They did tend to marry each other's money, meet at the Club, cultivate tennis and bougainvillea, attend chamber concerts and 'preserve standards' in quaintly Victorian ways.

An ardent spirit like Thistle, with her memories of 'merry days in 'Frisco' and her Byronic urges, must have found them hard to live with.

Did *Arcadian Adelaide* achieve anything beyond a spate of pamphleteering and excess adrenalin? Probably not. Nearly six decades of wowserism were still to come in 1905. But I am sure Thistle would approve of the current relaxed Adelaide, with its culture, heritage agreements and wine-with-everything. We tend, however, to forget the recent origin of this pleasant lifestyle. As late as June 1960, I.I. Kaven could lament in the *Australian Quarterly* that the new Festival of Arts was spoiled by 'the archaic laws and customs which prevail in South Australia. The dead Sundays, the six o'clock closing time on weekdays, the comparatively poor gastronomic achievements and notable shortage of good hotels, restaurants and night clubs make the visitors' life at the Festival difficult and, at times, tedious.'

Why reprint *Arcadian Adelaide*? I chanced upon *Arcadian Adelaide* while writing a history of Adelaide and found its wit and polemics a bracing and informative diversion from the masses of self-congratulatory civic and state publications I had had to ingest. The book and its author deserve to be rescued from the oblivion to which they had been so rapidly consigned by the rattled Arcadians.

For the time and place, Thistle was an original. Writing, when that was one of the few means of self-expression available to women, in a noble and courageous way, she broke the deafening silence of Adelaide self-criticism. For all its excesses, *Arcadian Adelaide* tells some home truths about the good old days. It, and the storm it provoked, tells us much about the way we were.

Finally and palpably, in an era outstandingly short of it, Thistle had fun. We hope that you have fun reading *Arcadian Adelaide,* and will agree that, along with colonial artefacts and architecture, Thistle Anderson deserves restoration.

Derek Whitelock (1985)

Illustrations sourced from

Wakefield Press is an independent publishing and
distribution company based in Adelaide, South Australia.
We love good stories and publish beautiful books.
To see our full range of books, please visit our website at
wakefieldpress.com.au
where all titles are available for purchase.
To keep up with our latest releases, news and events,
subscribe to our monthly newsletter.

Find us!

Twitter:
www.twitter.com/wakefieldpress
Facebook:
www.facebook.com/wakefield.press
Instagram:
instagram.com/wakefieldpress

Printed in Australia
AUHW022044101220
338235AU00006B/6